SCHIRMER'S LIBRARY
OF MUSICAL CLASSICS

Vol. 2111

PIANO MASTERWORKS

UPPER INTERMEDIATE LEVEL

97 Pieces by 20 Composers

ISBN 978-1-4950-0690-6

G. SCHIRMER, Inc.

DISTRIBUTED BY

7777 W. BLUEMOUND RD. P.O. BOX 13819 MILWAUKEE, WI 53213

www.musicsalesclassical.com
www.halleonard.com

CONTENTS

(Continued on next page)

ROBERT SCHUMANN

ALEXANDER SCRIABIN

PYOTR IL'YICH TCHAIKOVSKY

Invention No. 3
in D Major

Johann Sebastian Bach
BWV 774

Invention No. 6
in E Major

Johann Sebastian Bach
BWV 777

French Suite No. 5
in G Major

Johann Sebastian Bach
BWV 816

Allemande
Allegretto (♩ = 80.)

Courante

Allegro (♩=132)

Sarabande

Andante cantabile (♩=84)

14

Gavotte

Un poco vivace ($\half = 88$)

Bourrée

Allegro ($\half = 96$)

Loure
Moderato (♩ = 126)

Gigue
Vivace (♩. = 76)

Prelude
in G minor

Johann Sebastian Bach
BWV 930

Prelude
in D minor

Johann Sebastian Bach
BWV 935

Prelude
in E minor

Johann Sebastian Bach
BWV 938

Sonatina

I. Bagpipe

Béla Bartók

II. Dance*

Moderato (♩ = 80)

* In the 1950 edition, Bartók retitled this movement, "Bear Dance."

III. Finale

30

Bear Dance

from *Ten Easy Pieces*

Béla Bartók

L'enjouée

(The Light-hearted Maiden)
from *18 Characteristic Studies*

Johann Friedrich Burgmüller
Op. 109, No. 6

Les bohémiens

(The Gypsies)

from *18 Characteristic Studies*

Johann Friedrich Burgmüller
Op. 109, No. 4

La source
(The Spring)
from *18 Characteristic Studies*

Johann Friedrich Burgmüller
Op. 109, No. 5

Refrain du gondolier

(The Gondolier's Refrain)

from *18 Characteristic Studies*

Johann Friedrich Burgmüller
Op. 109, No. 14

Les sylphes

(Sylphs)

from *18 Characteristic Studies*

Johann Friedrich Burgmüller
Op. 109, No. 15

La séparation

(Parting)

from *18 Characteristic Studies*

Johann Friedrich Burgmüller
Op. 109, No. 16

Marche

(March)
from *18 Characteristic Studies*

Johann Friedrich Burgmüller
Op. 109, No. 17

Allegro maestoso (♩ = 144)

La fileuse

(At the Spinning Wheel)

from *18 Characteristic Studies*

Johann Friedrich Burgmüller

Op. 109, No. 18

à Monsieur Johns de la Nouvelle-Orléans

Mazurka

in B-flat Major

Frédéric Chopin
Op. 7, No. 1

à Monsieur le Comte de Perthuis

Mazurka
in G minor

Frédéric Chopin
Op. 24, No. 1

Mazurka
in A minor

Frédéric Chopin
Op. 67, No. 4
(Posthumous)

Nocturne
in C minor

Frédéric Chopin
KK. IVb, No. 8

Andante sostenuto

58

à J. C. Kessler

Prélude
in E Major

Frédéric Chopin
Op. 28, No. 9

à J. C. Kessler

Prélude
in C minor

Fréderic Chopin
Op. 28, No. 20

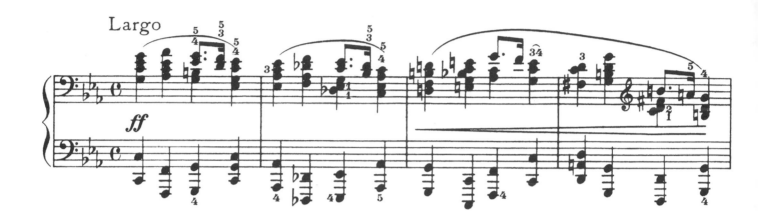

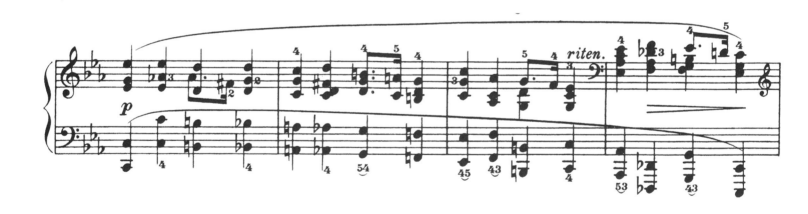

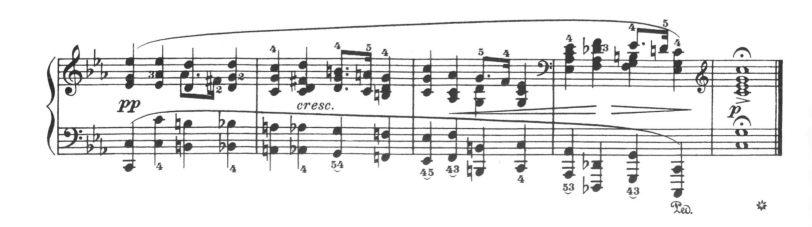

à J. C. Kessler

Prélude
in D-flat Major
"Raindrop"

Frédéric Chopin
Op. 28, No. 15

Sostenuto

Waltz
in B minor

Frédéric Chopin
Op. 69, No. 2
(Posthumous)

67

Waltz
in A minor

Frédéric Chopin
KK. IVb, No. 11

Allegretto

Waltz
in E-flat Major

Frédéric Chopin
KK. IVb, No. 10

Sostenuto

Children's Corner
I. Doctor Gradus ad Parnassum

Claude Debussy

Animato ma non troppo

72

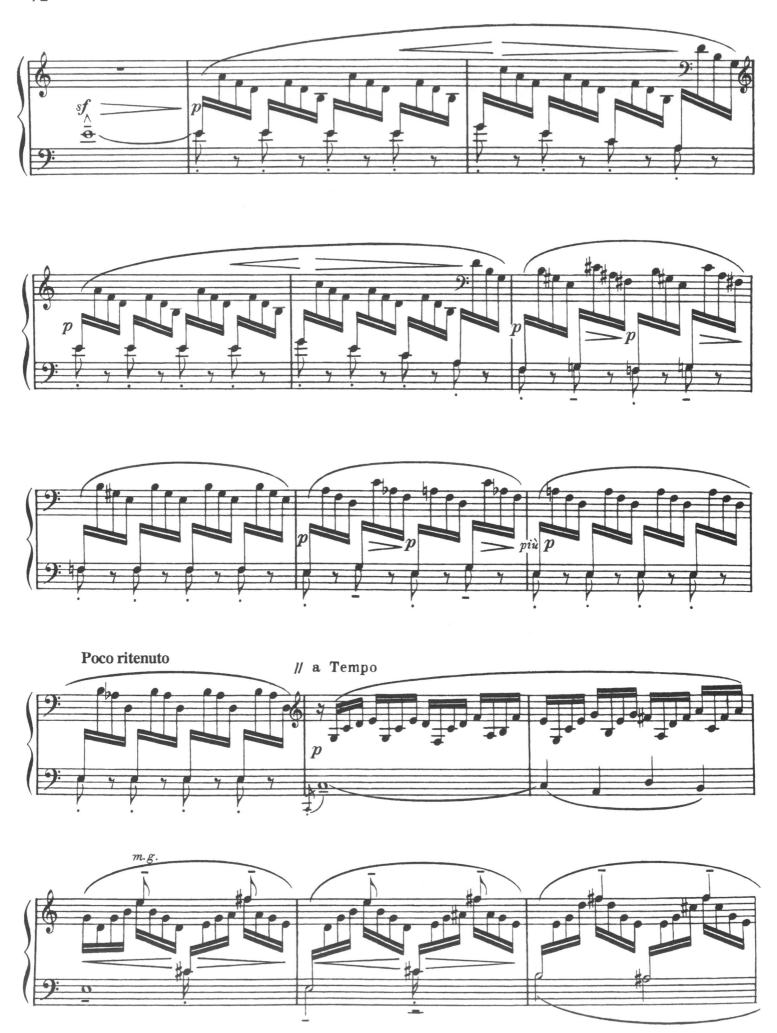

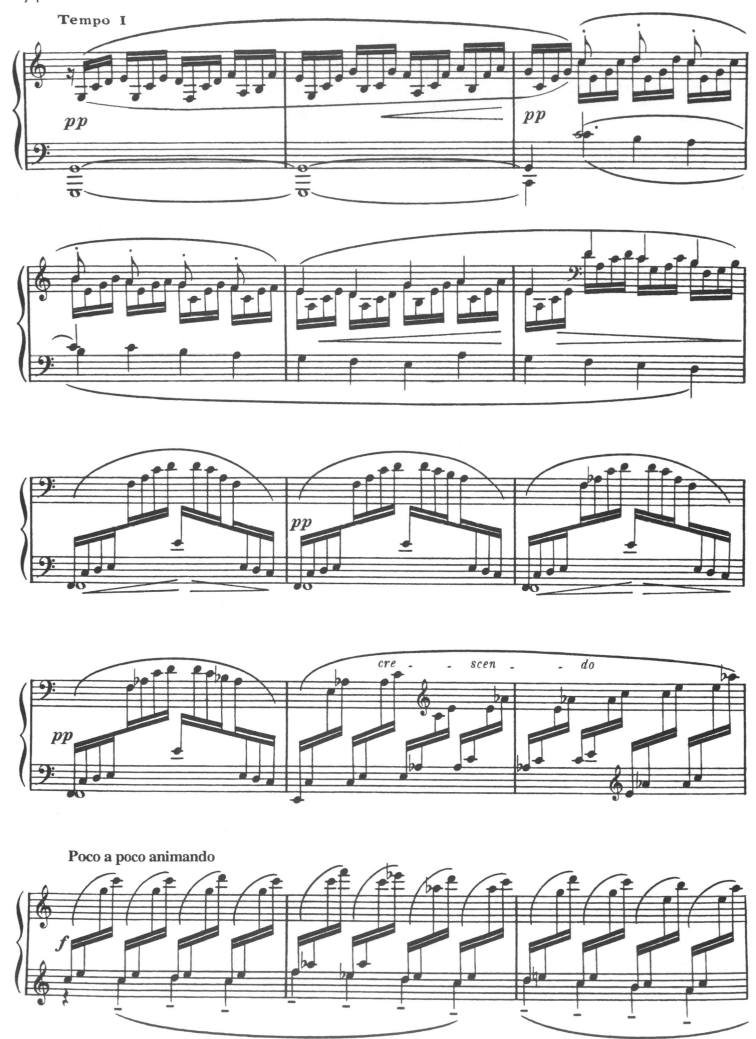

Molto animato

II. Jimbo's Lullaby

III. Serenade for the Doll

82

Tempo I

Senza rallentare

84

IV. The snow is dancing

V. The little Shepherd

VI. Golliwogg's Cake-walk

Arabesque No. 1
from *Two Arabesques*

Claude Debussy

Tempo rubato *(un peu moins vite) (somewhat slower)*

Rêverie

Claude Debussy

Le petit nègre

Claude Debussy

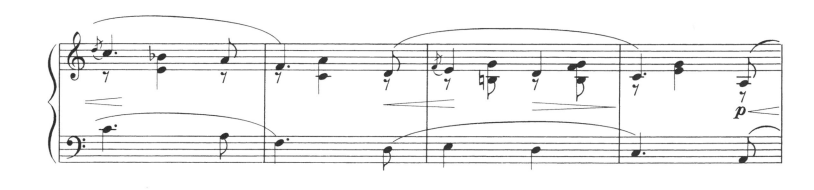

Des pas sur la neige

from *Préludes*, Book 1

Claude Debussy

Nocturne
in E minor

John Field

March of the Trolls

from *Lyric Pieces*

Edvard Grieg
Op. 54, No. 3

Notturno
from *Lyric Pieces*

Edvard Grieg
Op. 54, No. 4

Sailor's Song

from *25 Melodious Studies*

Stephen Heller
Op. 45, No. 14

Poco maestoso

Warrior's Song
from *25 Melodious Studies*

Stephen Heller
Op. 45, No. 15

Consolation No. 3

from *Consolations*

Franz Liszt

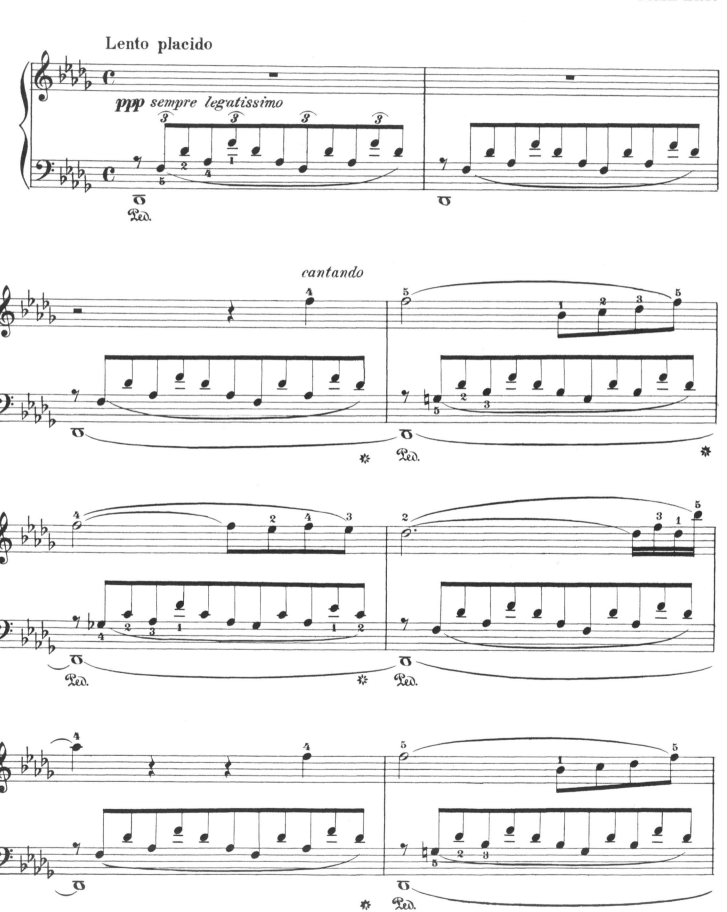

133

Four Little Piano Pieces

1

Franz Liszt

2

3

4

To a Water Lily

from *Woodland Sketches*

Edward MacDowell
Op. 51, No. 6

In dreamy, swaying rhythm ♩ = 52

The accompaniment very softly throughout

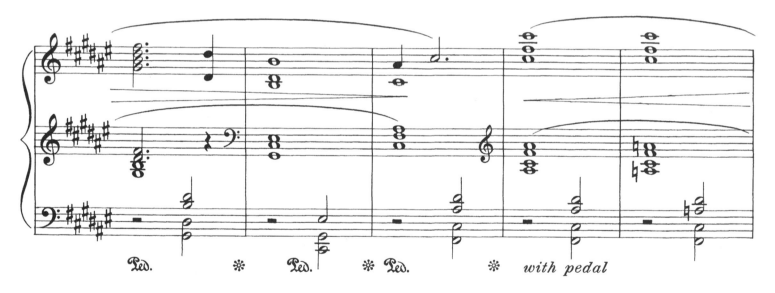

with pedal

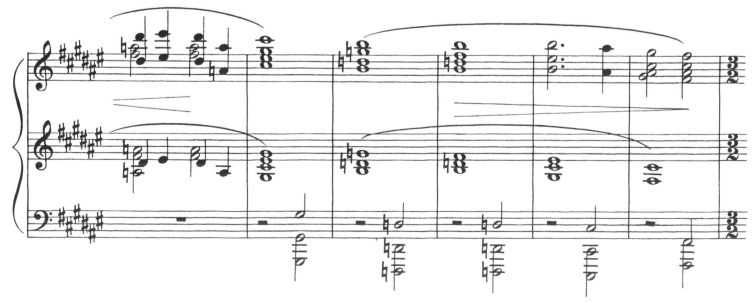

146

Shadow Dance
from *12 Etudes for the Development of Technique and Style*

Edward MacDowell
Op. 39, No. 8

This Etude is to be studied ***ppp*** - with the wrist high and without lifting the fingers high absolute equality both in tone and time is necessary.

148

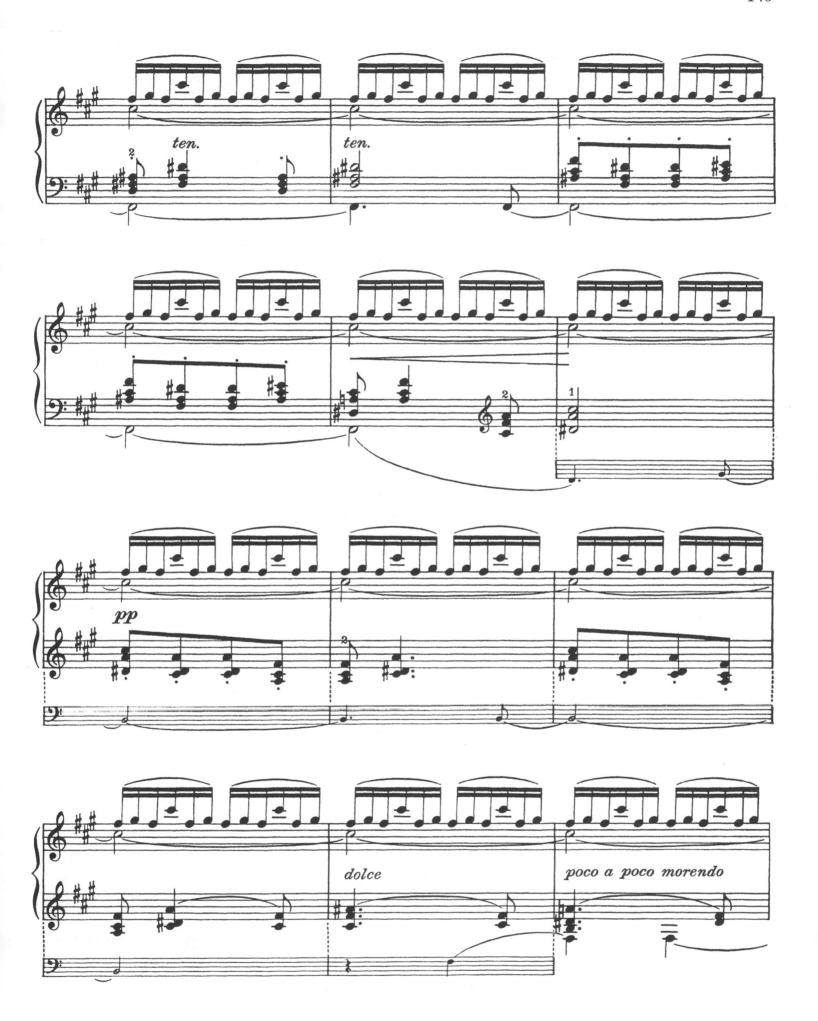

Song Without Words
in A minor

Felix Mendelssohn
Op. 19, No. 2

Andante espressivo (♩ = 120)

Song Without Words
in G minor
"Venetian Boat-Song No. 1"

Felix Mendelssohn
Op. 19, No. 6

Song Without Words

in F-sharp minor
"Venetian Boat-Song No. 2"

Felix Mendelssohn
Op. 30, No. 6

Allegretto tranquillo

Song Without Words

in E Major

Felix Mendelssohn
Op. 19, No. 1

a)
b) } Imitation of the preceding melodic phrase in the r.h.

Scherzino
from *Ten Small Pieces*

Moritz Moszkowski
Op. 77, No. 2

Tarentelle

from *Ten Small Pieces*

Moritz Moszkowski
Op. 77, No. 6

Suite No. 5
in C Major

Henry Purcell

a) or 𝄿

Almand
Moderato

Courante
Moderato

Saraband
Sostenuto

Cebell (Gavot.)

a) or
b) or

a) or ⁀

Minuet

Riggadoon

★) omit.
a) or 〰 or omit.

Intrada

March
Moderato

a) or 𝓌

*) omit.

à Mademoiselle Jeanne Leleu

Prelude

Maurice Ravel

Sonatina
in C Major

Carl Reinecke
Op. 47, No. 1

Rondo
Vivace (♩. = 126)

for Roland Manuel

Gnossienne*
from *Three Gnossiennes*

1

Erik Satie

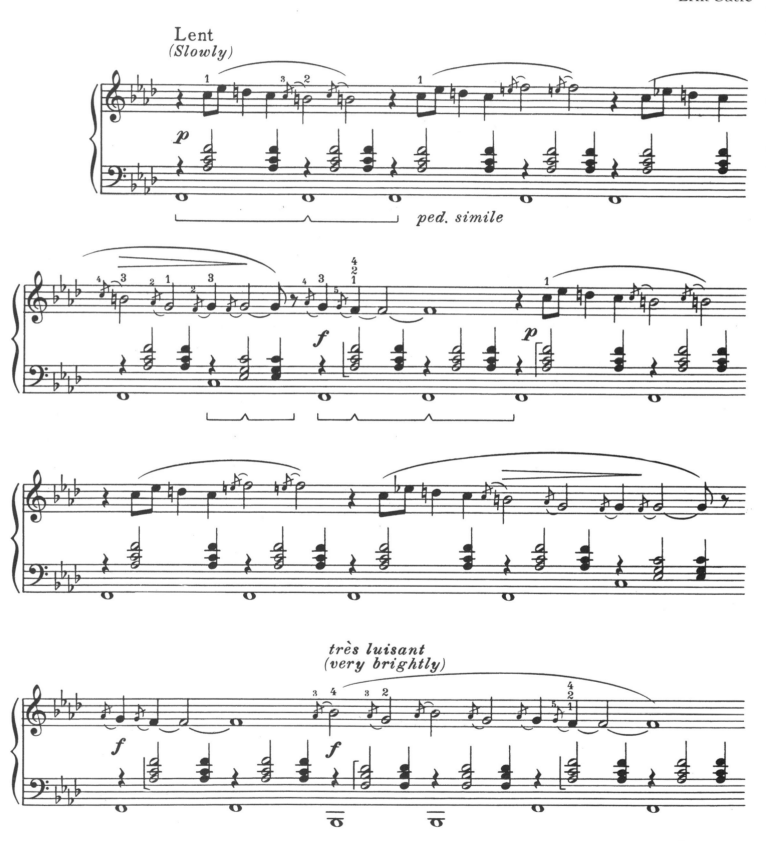

* The title is most likely a vague allusion to Cnossus, Knossos, or Gnossos, an ancient city on the island of Crete—the site of the palace of the mythical King Minos and the labyrinth where the Minotaur was confined— richly associated in ancient Greek mythology with Jupiter, Ariadne, and Theseus, the hero who slew the Minotaur.

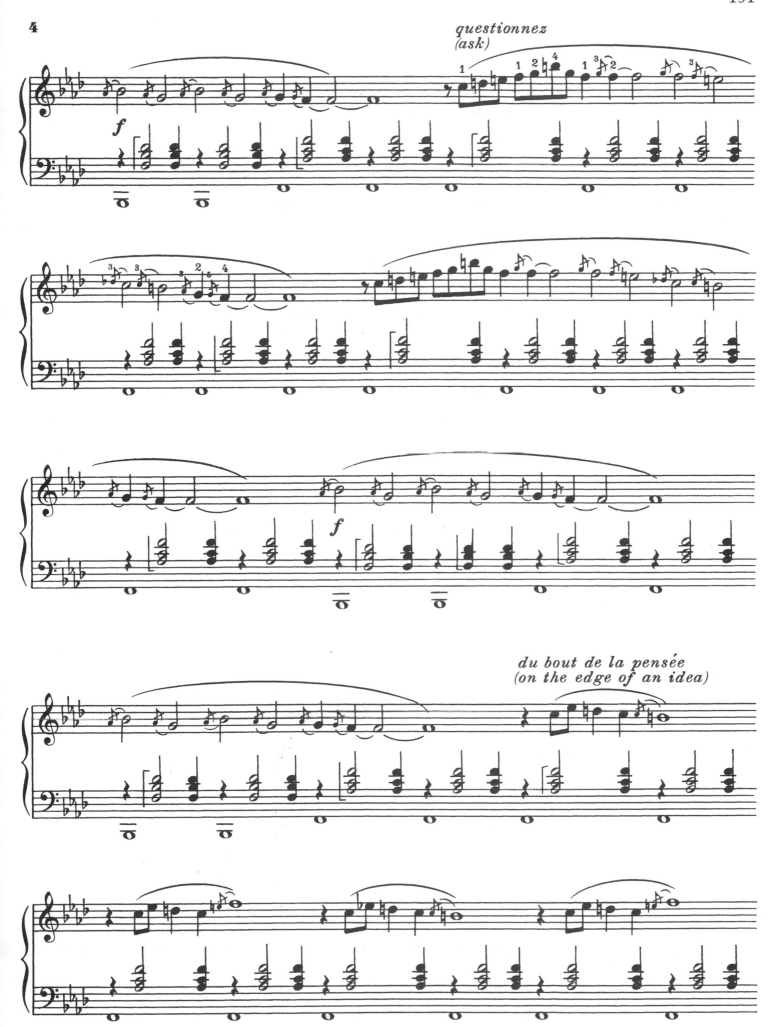

192

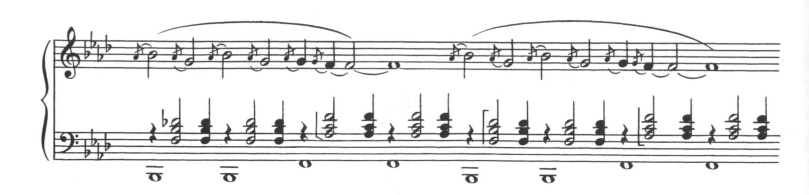

postulez en vous-même
(make your own demands)

pas à pas
(little by little)

sur la langue
(on the tip of the tongue)

à Mademoiselle Jeanne de Bret

Three Gymnopédies*

1

Erik Satie

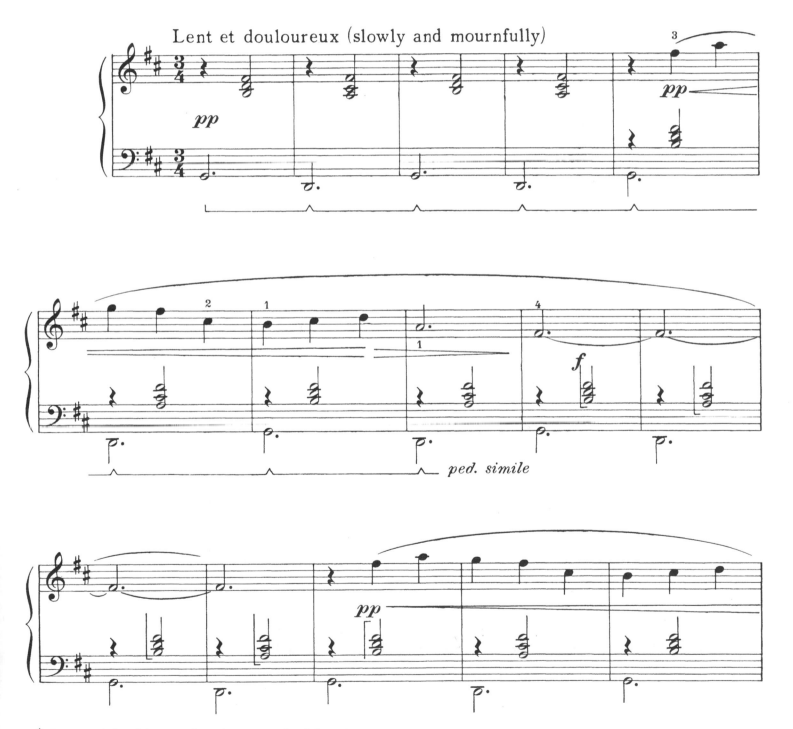

* Ceremonial choral dance performed at ancient Greek festivals.

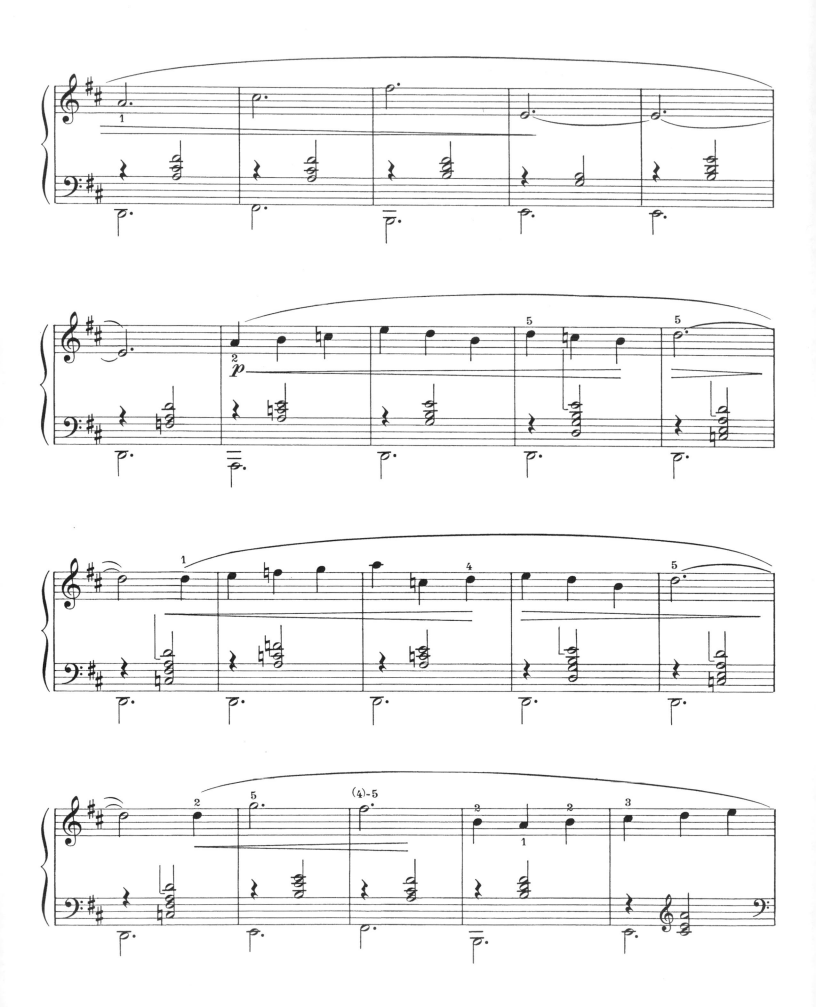

à Conrad Satie

2

à *Charles Levade*

3

Moment musicaux

in A-flat Major

from *Six moments musicaux*

Franz Schubert
Op. 94, No. 2

Moment musicaux
in F minor
from *Six moments musicaux*

Franz Schubert
Op. 94, No. 3

Allegro moderato (♩=96)

il basso sempre staccato

✳) May also be
played thus:

Moment musicaux

in A-flat Major

from *Six moments musicaux*

Franz Schubert
Op. 94, No. 6

Kuriose Geschichte

(Curious Story)

from *Scenes from Childhood*

Robert Schumann
Op. 15, No. 2

Bittendes Kind
(Pleading Child)
from *Scenes from Childhood*

Robert Schumann
Op. 15, No. 4

Glückes genug
(Perfectly Contented)
from Scenes from Childhood

Robert Schumann
Op. 15, No. 5

Wichtige Begebenheit

(Important Event)

from Scenes from Childhood

Robert Schumann
Op. 15, No. 6

Träumerei
(Reverie)
from *Scenes from Childhood*

Robert Schumann
Op. 15, No. 7

*Original

Am Kamin

(At the Fireside)

from *Scenes from Childhood*

Robert Schumann
Op. 15, No. 8

Ritter vom Steckenpferd
(The Knight of the Rocking-horse)
from *Scenes from Childhood*

Robert Schumann
Op. 15, No. 9

Kind im Einschlummern

(Child Falling Asleep)
from Scenes from Childhood

Robert Schumann
Op. 15, No. 12

Kriegslied
(War Song)

from *Album for the Young*

Robert Schumann
Op. 68, No. 31

Mignon

from *Album for the Young*

Robert Schumann
Op. 68, No. 35

Matrosenlied
(Sailor's Song)
from *Album for the Young*

Robert Schumann
Op. 68, No. 37

* **Execution :**

Prelude
in E minor

Alexander Scriabin
Op. 11, No. 4

Prelude
in G-flat Major

Alexander Scriabin
Op. 11, No. 13

The Hobby Horse

from *Album for the Young*

Pyotr Il'yich Tchaikovsky
Op. 39, No. 3

Chanson triste

from *12 Pieces*

Pyotr Il'yich Tchaikovsky
Op. 40, No. 2

Allegro non troppo

la melodia con molta espressione